The Safety of Sma

love Helen x

Selected Poems
by
Helen Whitten

orrydian

Copyright © Helen Whitten 2024
All Rights Reserved

No part of this book may be reproduced or stored in a retrieval system, or transmitted in any form or by any means, electronic, mechanical, photocopying, recording, or otherwise, without express written permission of the publisher.

www.helenwhitten.com

www.orrydian.co.uk

Contents

The safety of small things..1
Beyond the Senses..2
Population Explosion...4
#Bring Back Our Girls..5
The Economist...6
Serpentine Sunday 7
Norfolk Riverbank..8
Postcard from South America..11
Egypt's Shifting Sands: The Arab Spring, 2011.................................12
The Ring of Kerry...14
The Survivor..15
Poppy Centenary..16
On the Bed of Pansies..18
Ghekko..19
After the Exhibition...20
The State of the World..21
Gifts Differing...22
On Hold...25
The Origami Master and Ziggy Stardust...26
St Luke's – Pillars of Continuity..28
Proud to be a woman..30
A Letter from Love..32
After Hamlet 34
Fate or Fortune..36
To Ben: and to those we only meet for a minute or two........................37
Courage...38
Lost..40
The Friendship of Women...42
Journey of Love...43
Buttered Toast...44
A new dawn..45
Covid: the opportunist 46
The Melody of Lockdown 48
Covid Loss...49
Waves in a Lockdown World..50
Our lawn in Lockdown...52
A Page of Haikus..53

Moondance 54
Road Trip...55
San Telmo Tango 56
Requiem in absentia...57
A bump in the road 58
Never Again 59
The Garden 60
Days of Darkness..61
Dig up the World 62
Silence..63
I lie in my bath 64
Summer evening in Kew..66
There's a lot of love about if you look for it......................67
The Dos and Don'ts of Poetry For a Teenager, from Vernon
Scannell, 1966..68
Frame-Change..70
Fantasy Life 71
The World has Changed, 2022..72
Anthology..73
About the Author..76

The safety of small things

It's the way I think of my mother
every time I lay a table
the way she taught me,
the routine of yoga exercises when I wake,
stretching daily, for over fifty years of my life.

It's chopping an onion
and wiping away the tear,
only to make the weeping worse.

It's soaking in a bath of warm scented water,
doing the washing up,
loading the dishwasher,
picking up a child from school,
chatting to a neighbour,
soothing a baby's cry,
hugging one's son,
feeding the cat
under his watchful arrogant eye.

It's going to the shops,
taking a walk in Kew Gardens
and watching a golden leaf
flutter in the wind,
within limitless skies.

In the safety of small things
we can shelter from the storms
that whirl and swirl
beyond our gates.

(published in Orbis 204, 2023)

Beyond the Senses

In London's multi-channel streets
of reverberation, neon and technicolour,
we pass through the day

our eyes watching out
painting their pictures,
a pixillated interpretation

of colours and places,
blurred confusion around
the thin-lined focus

of the next task,
laptop leadening the step
eyes deep in the gutter

sharply drawing us
to blindness of the scene,
easily missing

the heart of the matter.
How much we see
of the young girl's sadness,

the old man's weariness,
the wrinkles or the dimples,
or the tiny pink buds

on the plant that winds up the wall.
Ears tune to the street cacophony
of sirens, cars, mobiles and planes,

the whispers of wind and voices fading
into the buzz and boom of earphones
next to us on the tube.

How much do we hear
behind the sound of church bells,
beneath words softly spoken,

beyond a young man's strutting laughter,
or the crash of a slamming door,
Do we catch the true notes of the tune?

Population Explosion

There's a population bubble
filling the streets,
bursting the Embankment,
lining along Knightsbridge,
circling the Gherkin,
mountaineering Primrose Hill.

Multiple wheels and pedals,
gleaming hubs and chains
everywhere you look.
Lycra gilets and leg warmers
so tight it's embarrassing.
It's not just the cracks in the pavement you notice.

There's no room on the crossing.
The multiplying cavalry attack from all sides.
Toddlers are hauled out of the way
of the marauding troops
seconds from getting flattened by tubular tyres
or flung from carbon handlebars.

This artillery is serious business.
You don't mess with them:
you're always in the wrong.
No insurance, no registration, no test
but it's their territory.
Or so they think.

#Bring Back Our Girls

Fifteen Chibok girls stand in a line,
their faces sombre, eyes haunted,
expressions of the near-dead.
They mutter their names as if they are ghosts
"Maimuna Usman, Rifkatu Galang, Naomi Zakaria.."

These Christian girls have their heads covered,
dark robes drape over them like items of laundry.
What experiences are hidden beneath?
No hiding from their captors, no escape,
and no one's finding them.

It must be hard for them to believe:
where are their parents,
the troops with binoculars, infra-red detectors?
Would they imagine that Goodluck Jonathan
would deny their kidnap?

Abhorrent years when they should have been
giggling in their dormitories,
chatting about bras and periods,
exchanging dreams,
flirting shyly with first boyfriends.

Instead they are brainwashed into Islam,
held in Cimmerian jungles by fierce men,
forced to wear suicide vests,
pleasure their Boko Haram captors,
blow up a marketplace where their parents shop.

(2014)

The Economist

I walked past Robert Peston today,
dishevelled dark hair flopping over black specs,
that familiar voice pitching and tossing
like a shipwreck at sea.

He stood on the patch of lawn opposite the Houses of Parliament,
striped scarf snaked around his neck, soft shoes,
an unmistakeable figure, buffeted by a cold wind,
his interviewer indifferent to the rain or his discomfort.

I couldn't hear what he was saying
nor the questions being posed.
There was no one nearby, just me on my way home.
"See ya," he called to the cameraman as he closed,

pulled his jacket taut across his chest,
trod the soaked grass beside me.
And then he sighed,
a long slow release of effort and fatigue.

I wanted to say hello, to empathise,
say something simple like "has it been a long day?"
After all he's part of the family, lives in our sitting rooms, kitchens,
bathrooms.
But he walked into the dusk in silence and alone.

Serpentine Sunday

I daydream along the Serpentine.
The moor-hen's cry
rasps like an old man's cough.

I watch the swans
with wings like the Angel Gabriel,
glide over water rippling with sunglinting stars.

The Chelsea crowd walk their dogs
beside tree trunks ruched like satin curtains.
The parakeets screech above.

Steeple bells from north to south
ring out to the camera-laden tourists,
congregations of the world assembled in our city.

Across the park women
in their moon-pink bras
stagger home from their Breast Cancer night walk

exchange tired smiles
and drag sneaker-weary feet
through London's dawn-damp grass.

(published in South Bank Poetry Anthology 2017)

Norfolk Riverbank

The great crested grebe nonchalantly saunters along the river,
self-satisfied and comfy in his feathered skin, mate and young by
  his side.
His crested plume is slicked like a young man's gelled Mohican.
He shakes droplets from his neck, preens his feathers.

Diving into the water, he catches his family's breakfast in the
  glutinous depths.
One slim silver fish after another slivers and thrashes in his long
  beak.
Fluid as mercury, the prey is passed into tiny yawning bills.
The small striped heads dip and turn as they gulp down the
  offering.

Beside them a family of ducks, a drake and his mate and ducklings,
paddle along the River Bure, spiralling reeds and wetlands.
A film of dawn mist still hovers over the surface and, in the
  marshes,
a swan sits on the nest amid swamp bush and petrified bark.

Coots and moorhens call across the stretch of Broad.
Cruisers, sailboats, dinghies seesaw as holidaymakers rig and rope.
The smoke of frying bacon draws optimistic goslings alongside.
An elderly wooden yacht slides by, tall mast and full sail,
  mahogany and brass glinting.

On board our boat a thimble of dandelion drifts onto the deck;
a gang of midges bustle and circle in random dance.
Along the bank a young deer fidgets and jumps shadow ditches,
foraging in the marshes beside the dyke.

Herds of brown cattle munch and move in a line across the flat
    landscape of patchwork field
as they have for millennia. The harriers hover above them.
A heron rises from his statue post in the reeds
to swoop and dive magnificent and triumphant over the river for his
    lunch.

The silence of the centuries sits in the land of fens.
Windmills turn slowly and the ancient stones of St Benet's Abbey
conjures up images of monks, intrigue between Henry VIII and a
    Bishop of Norwich;
a sense of footsteps of ghosts within the flint under my sneakers.

Henry's deluded determination nonetheless left this the only
    religious house open.
Dissolution eluded the monastery. Perhaps through dodgy-dealing,
    Bishop became Abbot.
Today's current incumbent still preaches an annual service on the
    first Sunday of August,
standing in the bow of a wherry as his minions lower the anchor
    into mud.

The hermit monks abandoned their inaccessible monastery through
    the stone gatehouse.
It stands supported by a farmer's addition of brick wind pump.
Tired by trudging and sailing miles for provisions, one by one they
    left,
buildings were demolished and all that remains are listed ruins and
    stones.

On the bank serenity seeps beneath my skin as I merge into nature's
 habitat.
Whispers of long-dead peat workers, fishermen and villagers slip
 into my ear,
with an awareness of the remoteness of lives contentedly cut off in
 their own small cosmos,
like a fingertip touch of balm, a reprieve from 21st century life.

Postcard from South America

I paid homage at Evita's Recoletta grave,
saw more poverty in the favelas
than you'd meet on an English street,
watched supple sexual acrobatics
at a tango show in Buenos Aires,
nearly died at the hands of a taxi driver
on a Lewis Hamilton suicide mission,
sat in the flea market in San Telmo
lilted by two guitarists in perfect tune,
heard stories of robberies and car-jackings,
corruption in high places,
drug gangs, violence and desperation,
an economy hit by recession,
heard the roar and thunder of the Iguazu Falls,
dazed by butterflies with mathematically perfect designs,
walked the beach at Ipanema,
seen a thousand lights of the favelas twinkle
brighter than the lives inside,
stood awed under Christ the Redeemer's pinnacle statue,
felt his compassionate influence over a troubled city,
driven a lethal road from Rio
past mile upon mile of half-house homes of desolation,
glassless windows, breezeblock walls, corrugated iron roofs,
dodged the barefoot boys beating motorway traffic
to a backdrop of mountain forest, sugar beet and palms,
seen tiny monkeys turn their noses up at bananas
that a hungry child might welcome.
I'll smuggle an essence of vibrant warmth home,
leave them their intimacy with a wilderness that we don't share,
return to the safety and orderly comforts we take for granted.

Egypt's Shifting Sands: The Arab Spring, 2011

I've stood in Tahrir Square,
felt the dusty heat,
done deals on street corners
with scruffy boys
adept at currency arithmetic,
seen the Pyramids at sunset
after the inevitable visit to a papyrus shop,
taken a horse
into the deserted dusk desert,
just me and a stranger,
hoof meeting sand at speed,
watched a solitary camel rider leering up
like a mirage from the tombs,
grabbing at my reins,
his smile lecherous as a snake.
The Sphinx watched it all.

And Tahrir Square that spring
was full of banners,
no Pharoah there,
no Rameses or Akhenaton,
just families gathering,
and a herd of colts
kicking their heels,
booting out the old folk.
Danton and Havel
on ghostly watch
as a velvet wave upturns
the status quo along
the banks of the glittering Nile,

centuries of despotic old men's decrees
unravelling like papyrus
from Tunisia to Syria.

Today, parched bones of camels
lie in dust hollows,
beside the looters' tunnels,
where antiquities feed
a desperate generation
in the land where
few tourists go.
Horses stand in starving heat.
Young boys despair
of providing sustenance
for ailing parents or sisters,
as tombs are raided
and dynamited
below their feet.

Money changes hands
in the brotherhood of power,
A journalist risks her life
to tell the story,
as the cabal watch
and shoot at her car
to silence her.
What scrolls will be written
in the blood-red desert
of history's graveyard
alongside the Pharoah's beasts
and treasures?
The Sphinx watches and waits.

The Ring of Kerry

Laughter ripples like a giggle in puffs of wind through the grasses
   of Kerry,
dances across crags and bright waters of the wild Atlantic Sea
with a mischief that teases the purple heathers, yellow gorse,
and slips into the banter of ever-chattering Irish lips.

It's a land of moors and streams, hills and valleys,
of dark peat bog holding the centuries in air and black water.
A mellow fiddle plays the landscape in one's ears,
moves tears to slide the sorrows down one's cheek.

Goats fearlessly climb grassy precipices above tiny white cottages,
their hooves catching a grip on ancient stones and boulders.
Gannets swoop and call from the sheer black rocks of Skellig
while greedy gulls reel timeless over the Cliffs of Mohan as we
   travel North.

In the pub the ageing fiddler taps his foot to a meandering jig,
a slow air calling to winking rogues and gypsies in the highlands.
A young girl's song skates the hilltops, skims down tiny white
   waves of surf,
whispering mysteries deep into smuggler's caves off Ireland's
   rebellious coast.

The Survivor

"I must live life to the full,
my brother died you see.
I can't waste a moment at all,
The fact is, he was only three."

But his wife and his team fell apart
through his driving and striving obsession.
He could never sit still or be quiet;
lost any true sense of compassion.

It took a crisis of ill-health
to make him stop and think
that far from creating wealth
he was driving himself to the brink.

He learnt to savour the moment,
to notice the dew on the grass,
to sit and quieten the ferment,
live slowly and let the guilt pass.

Poppy Centenary

From the mud of Flanders' fields,
hell-raised by Napoleon's troops,
earth-churned by hundreds of horses' hooves,
the poppies are calling,
the seeds of red bursting from disturbed ground,
a sea as scarlet as the blooded bodies
that rotted beneath their blooms.

From the clay ceramic petals are crafted
884,246 flowers, wire-stemmed,
as stiff as each skeleton remembered,
planted in London's moated earth
by volunteer hands
whose boots squelch
beside the rain-soaked Tower.

From the dungeon tunnels crowds emerge
amid megaphones of officialdom
taking up arms to warn of dangers,
halt tubes, stop traffic.
Still the poppies' silent call
draws thousands to tread their path
towards the poppy canyon.

From the Weeping Window
across snaking causeway walkways,
there is a blanket hush
as silent as London's awestruck grief
in Diana's Kensington Gardens,
each adult and child dumbfounded
by the scale of death remembered.

From the runway at Camp Bastion,
troops line to leave Afghanistans' opium fields,
their flack jackets and helmets,
hiding pain on their faces,
trauma in their eyes,
leaving four hundred and fifty-three ghosts of comrades
in smouldering hot desert dusk.

From the Tower, history stands watching
its bloody litany of wars and beheadings,
death masks from cruel centuries
of torture and public hangings,
flickering Youtube images
of helpless axed victims
of Isis' black-balaclava barbarism.

From the skies, birds flock down
in uncommon swoop across stone ramparts,
as if called by muted military bugle
to give thanks to lost lives, battle-sacrificed.
"You feel you have to come"
say the four million poppy-watchers,
as if mustered from beyond the grave.

(2014)

On the Bed of Pansies

Spring scent drifts into my ear
I lie on the kaleidoscope mosaic
a mattress softer than goosedown
purple petals entwine my hair
yellow flowers drip like earrings
pink velvet scarves around my neck
I sink drowning into the tapestry quilt
like Ophelia in a psychedelic blanket.

(The Belvedere Gardens in Spring, Vienna 2012)

Ghekko

The ghekko sits in the midday sun;
suave nonchalance in the tropics.
Noel Coward has nothing on him.
Silence is his subtle song.
Head held high,
coat-tail elegant,
he awaits his meal,
no mad dogs in sight.
He'll be served fly-pie
or ant caviar
on a silver-tongued platter,
as gracefully as if
it were the Savoy Grill.

After the Exhibition

It's raining as I come out of the tube,
pick a path across Trafalgar Square
through an anonymous blur of faces, ill-defined,
a broken jigsaw of eyes, noses, chins and cheeks,
to jostle through the doors of the National Portrait Gallery.

I shake the drops from my umbrella,
join the surging scramble for the entrance,
encounter a hush of critical scrutiny,
elbowed intent within polite smiles of the London crowd,
battle the throng to ponder the photographs.

I gauge the medium on the panelled screens,
absorb a miscellany of faces following my gaze,
features I might walk straight past
were it not for the particular moment of capture
that holds me mesmerised to their story.

The common facets we all share
caught in the lens of Annie Leibovitz:
celebrity, royalty, sports stars, tramps,
the extraordinary made ordinary, the ordinary extraordinary,
each wrinkle and contour an illustration of a life.

I recall St Petersburg, the Hermitage,
Rembrandt's perfectly crafted portraits ill-lit,
the elderly man with blue-veined pallid skin and watery eyes,
invisible had I crossed him on the street
made remarkable by art, history on his face.

I navigate through the swell of riveted onlookers,
everyday people suddenly made exceptional
as my eyes track the room with a sharpened viewfinder.
I walk back out onto the rain-drenched pavement,
down steps to the tube, knowing faces will never look humdrum
   again.

The State of the World

Does anybody know what they're doing?
The world is in chaos, the markets in a spin,
the jobs are disappearing, the debts are accruing:
doesn't anybody understand the mess we are in?

The Chinese are gloating, the Americans squabbling,
the Greeks are rioting, the British looting,
the Germans are disapproving, the French fretting
but the Italians just keep going bonga-bonga.

The economists differ, the Heads of State bicker,
first there are cut-backs then we're told to spend,.
Gaddafi and his dictators watch on and snicker
but will the million-dollar pensions never end?

The merry-go-round keeps a-turning
But nobody really knows what they're doing.

(24 August 2011)

Gifts Differing

For what it's worth ...
pay attention to your love
it's the silent breath of air between you
and languishes when neglected.
Simple to imagine the work meeting matters more
than coming home for dinner.
But easier to find work than love.

For what it's worth...
don't make love a battleground
or try to prove
you're right, the other wrong.
There are many roads and views.
Be flexible and listen:
don't enter the power struggle.

For what it's worth...
talk and don't bottle up feelings
or wait for the explosion,
though an outburst is better than icy silence or pursed lips.
Take time each week to stop,
not judge, but reflect and share dreams
for love can rise above the bickering.

For what it's worth...
remember each day to soften
and touch one another with compassion
for another's struggle to make sense
of the world. Forgive a weakness
accept a quirk, acknowledge a sensitivity
and focus on giving not receiving.

For what it's worth...
remember who you are.

Be together enough but not too much
don't lose yourself or forget how to live.
Your bond requires two whole entities
to keep the seal of love
both close and elastic.

For what it's worth…
encourage one another.
Enjoy and support the differing talents,
interests and paths
without put-downs.
Help one another to feel confident
to face another day in the world outside.

For what it's worth …
Remember the rest of the world loses its shine
when there's unhappiness at home.
Keep fun in your hearts,
enjoy life together,
take holidays, be spontaneous,
keep the romance alive.

For what it's worth...
bring a child into the world for its own sake not yours.
Don't tussle for position or who loves more.
There's no perfect way to raise children,
each parent brings differing gifts
that add value to life's unique journey.
Family creates a hub for love.

For what it's worth...
know that love will change
and there will be difficulties, conflicts,
sadness or alienation intervening as the years progress.
Work together in acceptance,
keep love in your voice,
transforming isolation into intimacy.

For what it's worth...
ask for what you need.
No-one knows what's inside your mind:
so don't hold things back
that impact others. Be courageous,
share your doubts, fears, uncertainties and dreams,
for it will bring you closer.

For what it's worth ...
dream up the life you both want.
Share the vision of the destination points
so your journey's compass
draws you forward
in the same direction,
propelled by shared values.

For what it's worth...
don't fritter love away,
or let complacency or neglect enter the home.
Think each day of one thing
that feeds and waters your connection
for if you have love
remember that it's fragile.

For what it's worth ...
keep laughter in your hearts,
music in your ears,
find fun in the small things
and keep smiling at the foibles –
your own and theirs!

On Hold

He's listening to music again,
repeating his name, patient number, birthdate, postcode,
then lost in another hour of Vivaldi's Four Seasons.
It's taken him four hours but still no outcome,
no likelihood of an appointment for another six months …
but "hang on", they say, "we'll see what we can do".
They click a few more switches, click off into the wilderness
of more musack until a new voice asks
"name, patient number, birthdate and postcode?"
and so the merry-go-round of the NHS continues.
Is there anyone there?
Does anyone care?

The Origami Master and Ziggy Stardust

It started with an ending.
Brixton one bleak January day.
Fans came to revere the rock star
turned to stardust and ashes.
Flowers and tributes jammed the wet London streets.
As the pandemonium hushed, summer moments later,
a young man arrived. "Let's build a wall" he said,
"cover it with origami wishes to honour the starman".

The dreams flew in on origami wings,
whispering their messages to the morning's wind.
They were cut and crafted with sharp edges,
squares, circles and triangles,
pleats of hills and valleys
that let the light in,
leaving space for the unknown.
Each fold touched with creativity.

As they landed on the frame they multiplied
into many-coloured shapes of intent.
A chatter of paper wishes
red warming green, purple brushing blue
into sacred blends of hope,
orange burnishing cream and white like a hot desert sand,
silver glittering like coins,
gold as warm as honey.

The origami master drew them in
from distant ends of the earth
with their pencils, pens, paintbrushes, scissors,
each paper folding
into tiny cranes, butterflies and flowers,
mini sculptures with handwritten notes
in French, English, Chinese, Japanese,
some neat, some scribbled.

Once complete the origami fluttered
on a drifting air of voices,
cutting through dark storms and rain,
to cast silhouette shadows across still lakes
in the moonlight, like fragile birds in flight,
carrying dreams, some as comfortable as an armchair,
others jumping high on a cloud of peace or mountain of adventure,
each murmuring a reminder that we can all be heroes.

(Brixton, on the death of David Bowie, 2016, published in Orbis)

St Luke's – Pillars of Continuity

The church throngs with voices of welcome,
the Chelsea crowd arrive for eucharist and a baptism.
Children in their pristine tweed Sunday coats with velvet collars,
mothers in designer clothes smile benignly as they hold their
   babies.
Fathers wrestle with defiant toddlers attempting to maintain a
   sacred order.
Despite their city suits and chief executive status, these men are
   powerless and unprepared
as their child falls floppy or stands rigid, refusing to respond to his
   authority.
Negotiating with employees in their thousands would be so much
   simpler.
He cannot overcome the will of this small infant, however hard he
   tries.

Small girls sit pretty, their hair immaculate, tied up with pink bows.
The boys treat the pews as a climbing frame,
weaving under shelves and over chairs, running up and down the
   aisle.
The vicar and choir watch patiently as their church resembles a zoo
of sound and movement, squawks and tutting, hands grabbing
   collars.
The priests continue their prayers, hymns and sermon
and somehow I feel that their words of celebration and love
will seep through the minds of these small souls,
sewing memories of Christian words and music into their memory
   banks.

These spruced people recapture their own childhoods of middle
England,
savouring the continuity of ritual and practice, a community of
values,
many involved in charity and good works,
raising their rumbustious children in this uncertain world,
surrounding them with love - family, friends and a crowded
congregation
of husbands, wives, children, widows, widowers and divorcees.
The vicar talks of dramatic immersion to cleanse the baptised baby
and reminds us that we can, at any time of life, choose to begin
again
in faith, in newness of purpose. I walk out onto the chilly London
street, inspired.

Proud to be a woman

I'm proud to be a woman
with double X chromosomes,
breasts, womb and oxytocin.
I can leap over mountains
ride over hills
do maths, play cricket,
be an engineer
if I want to.
But I am woman,
my intuition guides me
along a path reason may not see.

I may lead a business or a country
perhaps differently to any man
with his XY chromosome and testosterone.
I am happy with that.
What I bring is different.
I catch the messages in the ether,
notice danger from the corner of my eye,
small details a man may not see.
I hear the sadness in a friend's voice,
the hunger in a baby's cry,
the loneliness in my mother's eye.

I still struggle to break through
but I won't to do it the same way as you.
I shall be my own woman.
I will walk alongside you
but never again one step behind
or down.
I'll tear down the barricades of perception,
brighten the blind eyes,
shout through deaf ears,
to celebrate my difference.
For my double X way is equal to any XY.

A Letter from Love

Dear ones, how can I ever live up to your expectations,
through the washing up and the drudgery,
nights of exhaustion from work or a baby's cry,
through the arguments of "I want to do this" "you want to do that"?

You have been sold a paradise none of you can live up to
and I ache with the pain of your disappointment.
There is no knight on a white charger, no prince or princess
living in the happily-ever-after.

I watch and notice how this promised land lingers through your
 lifetime
chipping away at the acceptance of your fallibility,
making you feel something is broken when perhaps it isn't,
that somewhere around a corner perfection lies.

You need to be wary of mistaken identity, not be lured by some
 imposter.
It is not me in your home if there is control, limitation or put-
 downs.
No part of me includes violence towards another.
If someone disguises themselves as me, find the open door.
 Escape.

But I am uplifted and not a little astonished by those of you
who turn towards one another again and again,
picking your way through the brambles of your lives,
holding out a hand to the one who stumbles or whose skin is torn,

waiting to realign, to look once more into one another's eyes
and say "I see you, the inner you",
those of you who accept the struggle and muddle of life's effort
with love, patience, kindness.

For this allows me in, not as an ideal of love
but in my true form – for who I am,
not the love of the fairy tales
but a deeper love that endures the tiny batterings of each humdrum
  day.

Your servant,
Love

After Hamlet …

To #MeToo or not #MeToo, that is my question.
Whether 'tis nobler for women to suffer stoically
the slings and arrows of outrageous male behaviour,
or to take arms against a sea of wandering hands
and oppose them to the end.

Do we die as victims or sleep no more
and end the heartache, and the thousand natural shocks
which female flesh is heir to?
Evil cannot consistently be ranked equivalently,
nor men be accused on social media without just trial.

To die, as some poor accused souls have already chosen,
or to sleep, perchance to dream of equal status. Ay, there's the rub.
For, in that sleep, what legacy may come to our granddaughters
when we have shuffled off this mortal coil? This must give us
    pause.
Be watchful, that none be bound unwilling in their apron strings.

.
For who need bear the whips and scorns of time:
th' oppressor's wrong; the proud man's sense of entitlement;
the pangs of humiliation; the law's delay for a body or name
    wronged;
the insolence of the locker room; the spurning
through Twitter or Facebook which signals false news?

Debate and action must speak with reason, not grievance nor
    revenge.
Don't let cyberbullies silence or make cowards of us but be
    resolute.
Don't confuse a wink or the hand on the knee for rape. Speak out
    fairly.
The enterprise of accusation must be contemplated with wisdom
    and justice;
don't lose the name Suffragette in misguided denunciation or
    reaction.

And do not dictate whether we can frolic in bikinis or act as
    hostesses if we choose;
stop us earning money if we enjoy the caper. We don't need
    another's protection
if self-righteous intention removes our freedoms and casts us
    backwards.
Heed, nobody speaks out for all women, because we are multitudes.
Don't limit us with safe spaces, no-platforming nor censorship.

Don't cast our eyes on minor ills where we can learn to say No.
    Firmly.
Look instead to change the excesses of misogyny and domination,
the practices sidelining our daughters from Government
or entrapping young babes with outdated cruelty.
Raise the power of female voices high, with dignity and with honor.

(Published in Orbis 186, 2018)

Fate or Fortune

Is the child born in a Delhi slum less fortunate
than the child born in a Belgravia mansion?
A woman born beautiful luckier
than one who can pass unnoticed in the street?

Is it lucky to be a prodigy,
born with music or art in their fingertips
or mathematics in their brain?
Or might expectations of these gifts become a burden?

We carry our lucky charms and superstitions
like talismen for protection
but can make our own luck
or have it tipped upon us in unexpected moments.

We can explore every corner
for a magic sign that luck will come our way
but live through wars or recessions
with little control beyond our own breath.

We can take care of our health
run, jump, swim and go to the gym
but be struck down by a cancer that
seeped into our body without warning.

The one who is disabled but can still smile
makes their own perception of good fortune
whereas another is burdened
by grief, sadness, victimhood or revenge.

To Ben: and to those we only meet for a minute or two

I only met you for a moment
but you left a mark
like a pawprint
on my memory.
We spoke of your life
and your troubles.
You were honest about the challenge
and a warmth of compassion
passed between us.
So whilst you have gone,
too young, too soon,
to another,
and hopefully more peaceful place,
you have left an imprint with me,
a sense of that meeting,
that will occupy a space
in my mind,
probably for ever.

Courage

Courage is a splintering of fear
mobilising muscle and sinew into battle,
conquering all thought of self
to brave the frozen wasteland of war.

Courage is taking the stage
to speak up for something you believe in
or share knowledge that could enrich life,
even in the face of derision and dissent.

Courage is putting your shoulder into work
despite hating every moment,
aching to the bone with exhaustion,
to put food on your family's table.

Courage is hearing the doctor's diagnosis,
biting down your fear,
continuing to make life good each day
through pain, medical invasion or limitation.

Courage is asking for help, accepting kindness,
giving power to those who support you,
stifling your pride to expose vulnerability,
inviting the gift of love to be given and received.

Courage is living with diverse people,
perceiving all living creatures as sacred,
free to sing their unique song,
however mysterious the music may seem to you.

Courage is stepping out each day
after loss, grief tearing at your heart,
a hollow in your gut,
all breath and movement a struggle.

Courage is living alongside the natural world,
slipping through waves, taming winds,
whispering to a horse through gentle hands,
speeding down snow or up mountains to reach a peak.

Courage is being yourself with authenticity,
having the wisdom to know who you are,
bypassing those who hurt you,
stepping into the light of your true self.

Lost

I stand alone
a dark sky above me
no path ahead.
The whisper of wind in the trees.

I have no name,
no word in my ear that is mine.
No connection to
past, present, future.

I don't know what my mother used to call me,
nor my husband, or friends.
I cannot remember nor recognise who I am.
One moment there, next wiped out.

The earth beneath my feet is firm
yet I am at sea
without an anchor.
Lost.

What's in a name?
A sound my parents enjoyed.
An association to others
who bore that name.

What am I without it?
A woman, yes, a mother,
A daughter, sister, wife, colleague, friend,
but there are many of those who walk beside me.

I have lost a name before.
My name changed on marriage.
The sound of it does not speak of my beliefs
or values, nor what I stand for.

It is just a word. But without it
I am invisible, untethered,
drifting I know not where.
Anonymous in the dark.

The Friendship of Women

If I could paint a picture of friendship
it would capture the warmth of women,
the way they know one another without words,
a knowing drawn from shared experience of the world.
The kindness of heart, attention of listening,
heeding the signs that intuit the authenticity of feeling
beyond the everyday response of "I'm fine",
the weariness of body at the end of a busy day,
the longing to have made all those whom she loves comfortable.
But how to depict the loyalty of a friend
valued in their ups and downs,
quirks and talents, skills and vulnerabilities?
Such things are hard to portray
for they are felt through the touch of a hand,
gentleness of a glance, hint of a smile.

Journey of Love

It starts with a kiss, a glance, a touch,
that journey of love, lust, chemistry.
Is it destiny that draws you towards someone
draws you away from another?

Until the lust has calmed
and you have travelled a few stops together
you do not know the destination.
You're travelling blind.

You do not know where you will arrive
or whether you will part
at a crossroads or the first bump along the way.
Some magnet keeps you there.

It could be hope or optimism.
It could be an old pattern of pain from childhood.
It could be a sense that you should make changes,
or it could be revenge to hurt another.

But when you have travelled across difficult terrain,
stopped to choose together the next turning,
accepted one another's foibles and remain in step along the path,
that is, perhaps, the true journey of love.

Buttered Toast

The news arrived just as I was toasting bread
"another 3 weeks of lockdown".
Blast, I thought, we're out of Marmite
and, worse still, so is Ocado.

And so I clean the all-too-clean house
yet again
and notice how the floor has not been muddied
with children's footprints

nor the toys in the garage
taken out of their box.
I think of Toy Story
and wonder if they are lonely.

Perhaps they are as bored
as I am, perhaps as sad,
missing the voices, squabbles
and giggles.

By Kew Green the swing
rocks empty,
the slide a pristine steel
of no sticky fingerprints.

And so I butter my toast
and wonder how long it will be
before Ocado manage to source
the Marmite!

A new dawn

Great slicks of oil drift down the quiet river.
A narrowboat, smoke spewing from its funnel,
chugs its heavy load under autumn skies.
Beside the canal, frost glistens on branches,
frozen leaves crunch beneath my feet.
Ahead there's a clear blue sky,
a golden beam of sunlight
that brightens the pale morning and warms my heart.

Covid: the opportunist

Stealthily he moves through shadows.
Disenchanted with his rodent dwelling,
he's seeking new places to colonise.
Like a conquering Emperor
his eye roves new territory.
Without so much as a by-your-leave
he jumps into unsuspecting prey,
slithering from bat to snake to human,
slipping silently through the skin,
invading the cells,
settling into cosy homes
of lung or throat,
cackling at his success,
flaying his enemy in days,
no weapons necessary
no armies, guns or swords,
just a mushrooming of intruders,
the occupying force
aiming to debilitate and kill
across borders, laughing at customs checks,
shifting seamlessly between one nation and the next,
no passport needed.
Like a thief he evades detection,
fools the x-ray security checks,
invisibility his trump card.
He can't believe his luck.
He has brought the world
to a standstill,
his victims isolated,
struggling for breath
exiled from touch.
He rampages through bodies.

There's no stopping him
leaving his mark
on door knobs, surfaces, handrails.
The scientists will get him in the end.
They usually do.
There will be no victory song
when he is eventually defeated,
finding himself homeless.
But we shall be on the lookout
for any future attack, surreptitious or direct.
We shall hope to be prepared.

The Melody of Lockdown

I reach my hand up to the sky
and touch a silence
soft as a silken spider's web.

The only sound, in blossom-laden trees,
are songbirds,
their twitter like a whisper in my ear

predicting, perhaps, this moment
when the world came to a halt
where grounded planes liberated the skies.

Atop a garden wall a child
smiles "one two three – whee"
and flies into the safety of his mother's arms.

Along the pavement a jogger's sneakers
beat a timpani drum roll,
accompanied by an orchestra of bees.

Past closed doors of shops and cafes
sadness, like a cello's lament,
plucks at my heart strings.

The melody of lockdown
stills on the air, numb with disbelief.
The conductor has left the podium.

Covid Loss

I cry for the world that was
Where people flew from place to place
Where cities bustled with life
Shops chirupped to the sound of money in their tils
Where people could wander free without masks
Where we did not look on one another as dangerous
Where politicians focused on the daily grind
And everyone was employed and had a future
Where doctors showed some interest in their patients
And babies were born with two parents present
And those who died were held by their loved ones in their dying
   hours
Where we didn't have to live in fear of those we loved dying
But could go about our days care-free
I cry for the world we have lost
And pray that it may return.

Waves in a Lockdown World

The sadness came in waves:
what had happened to my life,
the places I had known,
the family I could hug?
All of a sudden there was separation;
separation from all that was familiar,
isolation from those whom I loved.

The fear came in waves:
what would happen next?
Would I become ill, would my Type 1 granddaughter?
My sons in their 40s were supposedly low risk
yet I read in the paper of ICU nightmares.
And what of their jobs, their future, the world,
the economy, my shares and retirement pension?

The confusion came in waves:
the streets I had known clogged with traffic
now unrecognisable, empty of cars, buses, people,
a desolate world of buildings where people hid
talking to one another in little boxes on a screen,
with governments and health services equally bewildered,
knowing less not more about this illness that had hit the world.

The anger came in waves:
that journalists focused on blame and criticism,
every programme on radio, tv, discussing only one subject: Covid,
nothing else that happened in the world reported.
Mistakes made were the topic of conversation
little about the progress, lives saved, or the odd good decision.
How are we to feel optimistic with no balance of perspective?

The gratitude came in waves:
at neighbours who asked about our needs,
the NHS medics busy at their jobs,
the Ocado and Amazon delivery staff
dropping essentials on our doorstep,
our families and friends who Zoomed frequently
to make sure we were well and had all we needed.

The frustration came in waves:
why can't these global leaders cooperate instead of isolate?
Why do they claim to have the 'world-beating' solution as if a
competition?
Why not encourage an objective global investigation
to search out the causes of the pandemic,
how it happened, why and how to prevent it happening again?
Instead they bicker like children in a playground.

The courage comes in waves:
taking baby steps out of lockdown
to see people in person, get on a tube,
talk to friends in their garden, visit our families,
open the schools and acclimatize ourselves
to a world that inevitably and eternally has risks.
To reclaim our lives and hug our children once more.

Our lawn in Lockdown

A place for tea,
and tag
and hide-and-seek
(for stick insects or 4 year-olds).
A place to meet
at social distance
in lockdown
or toast a birthday,
giggle with girlfriends,
lie in the sun,
read a book,
have a picnic,
catch-up as a committee,
or just enjoy the blackbird
singing in the tulip tree
under a cloudless sky

A Page of Haikus

A white feather drifts
In fingertips of the wind
No haste, no hurry.

A robin calls us
From a winter's branch in Kew
"Stop and look" he sings.

Autumn leaves scatter
Beside the muddy puddles
Boys love to jump in.

The air is chilly
Lights sparkle around London
Christmas is coming.

Children write letters
Telling Santa their wishes
Dreams mailed to heaven.

A black cat is curled
Like a comma on my knee
Warm bundle of purr.

We wander confused
What does Tier 2 really mean
Shrug and kick the leaves.

Pink blossom adorns
Winter-flowering cherries
Brightness in the dark.

Moondance

I would love to dance among the stars,
sprinkle stardust over the earth,
light up minds and be-glitter hairstyles.
I would love to walk around the moon
feel its soft white moondust under my feet
like white sand between my toes,
melt into its surface so we are one,
and look down on earth and see this moonshine
brighten fields like daylight,
lighting the way through the dark woods,
like a spotlight on the stage of life,
picking out the rabbits and scuttling mice
running for shelter of burrows,
escaping the foxes.
I would like to see the wonder in so many eyes
shining with awe as I track across the sky,
see the effect a blue moon has on lovers
around the world, every month of every year,
yet always surprising, always amazing,
a magnetic invisible force drawing in the tides,
lighting white horses riding on dark waves.
On full moon nights
I flick a little lunacy into people's minds,
keep them from sleep,
pluck more babies from their watery wombs
with my intensity and power.
A steady circle
set within a tempestuous, clear or cloudy sky
here we'd be together sprinkling a little magic
from the North Pole to the South
from the East to the West
lighting the dark shadows
of the earth and mind
so all are moonstruck.

Road Trip

From Memphis to Nashville
We hit the open road
And there was music
Calling from the boondocks,
That country music
That gets you in the gut
So happy or sad
Just a musician telling a story
For all to share.

We walked the rooms of Graceland
Had the best night of our lives
At the Grand Ole Opry
Where men wore Stetsons
And women cried
At the innocence of life
In all its highs and lows
Transformed to song

San Telmo Tango

Two old guys sit in San Telmo Market.
They look at one another from time to time,
share a wink, a smile, a language
spoken through their fingers
and the notes rising from their guitars.

They sit on ancient wooden stools.
A granddaughter wanders over to listen,
sits next to her grandmother, who stands
as an elderly man crosses the square,
takes her in his arms for a tango.

For a moment the chords revive their limbs.
They dance across the flagstones,
her in her fishnet tights, badly dyed hair,
he, still elegant in bow tie, embracing
sensuality, gliding, sweeping, twisting, turning.

Around them colourful market stalls
sell crystal glass, cocktail shakers, plush linens,
symbols of another age, amid Argentine poverty,
the swirling couple draw the crowd
into their spicy seduction, dissolving time.

Just two old men and their guitars.

Requiem in absentia

There was no music at her funeral
but we could sense her there
as we had last seen her,
an 105 year-old figure,
stooped over her piano,
skinny neck sunk into her chest,
crooked fingers gnarled over the keys.
.

There was no music at her funeral
but for us she'd played Haydn,
her hands dancing in perfect form
"the songs of my childhood" she'd said,
then sang calypsos from Trinidad
lullabies she'd hummed to the Kinder children
she'd transported from Germany.

There was no music at her funeral,
just awkward quiet in the Quaker hall,
a shuffling of shoes on bare boards,
the odd cough, a fidget,
eyes that glanced up for a moment
then back to the floor.
And silence.

There was no music at her funeral.
An omission of sound.
Her life had been teaching young hands to play.
A choir should have sung,
an orchestra performed,
a fanfare heralded a farewell.
There was no music at her funeral.
(Prizewinner, Elmbridge Literary Festival Poetry Prize 2021,
published in Orbis)

A bump in the road

Death is just another bump in the road,
so the pastor said,
as if it were nothing, a tiny twist in one's life,
the turn of a corner, instead of oblivion.

The poets talk of just standing in another room,
not having disappeared from life,
as if we could simply open the door and walk back in,
shake the hands of those we love. But we can't.

The priests talk of never-ending life,
perhaps of returning in another body.
I wouldn't want to be an ant, might enjoy being my cat.
But we wouldn't remember the lessons we learnt.

The psychics talk of spirits surrounding us,
sitting on our shoulder, sharing their wisdom,
whispering which might be a good path to take,
which might not. But their words get lost in translation.

A bump. That doesn't sound so comfortable,
but equally the pastor isn't describing a crater,
nor a volcano. Just a little bump, a gentle nudge then, perhaps,
into another space none of us knows exists.

Never Again

Never Again,
That's what they said,
Those Holocaust survivors,
Who never wanted others to suffer as they did.

Never Again,
That's what they said,
The parents who lost a child through violence,
To ensure no other parents grieved as they did.

Never Again,
That's what they said,
As they towed away the car wreck,
And realized they had taken the corner too fast.

Never Again,
Is what they said in 1945,
When all who had lived under a dictator
Vowed they would never let an autocrat rise again

Never Again
Is what they said after Hitler, Stalin, Pol Pot, Mao Zedong.
We will not allow it,
Cannot tolerate it,
Will have ways to stop it.

Never Again,
We all said,
Will there be another World War
But then sat on our laurels,
Believing we had learnt the lessons

But had we ...?

The Garden

A seed planted itself in her mind,
Fragile, yet bursting with life.
She nurtured it,
Watered it, kept it from the frost,
But a blizzard of snow
Fell one night
And she felt it had died
In the stone-cold ground.

She let it go, forgot it,
Other seeds replaced it.
She turned them over
In the depths of her dreams,
Yet they escaped into earth-dark crevices
Of wind-blown ideas,
Somewhere
just out of reach.

But, as the first buds of spring broke through,
The early sun warmed her,
Melted the icicles of her mind,
Cleared the pathways of winter's debris,
And there it was,
The original idea
She thought she had lost.
She took up her pen and wrote.

Days of Darkness

These are the dark days,
the days of rain
and cloud,
of snuggling under a duvet,
longing for spring.

These are the dark days,
when we pack up the Christmas tree,
carefully wrap the angel, the tinsel, into the old box
and hold the decoration one's child made at nursery
gently in the palm of our hand.

These are the dark days,
when the clouds hang low
over the trees and damp rooftops,
dawdling for a moment, then swirling
away in the wind.

These are the dark days,
where we need electric light even at midday,
but the glimpse of a rainbow
reminds us
there is still a sun up there somewhere.

These are the dark days,
when it's hard to lift our spirit
or feel joyful,
when the grey of the sky
mirrors the grey in our hearts.

These are the dark days
of waiting,
waiting for the end of frost and endless dusk,
waiting for the buds and that first streak
of light that heralds springtime.

Dig up the World

Dig up the world,
throw the hard earth
high in the air
where all those fixed beliefs
are scattered
among the whispers,
and the doubts.
And as they fall to earth
let them seed themselves
in new places,
green with hope,
where young flowers
will grow a fresh palate of colour
to spread love across the borders.

(Inspired by a line from The Place Where We are Right by Yehuda Amichai 1924-2000. Written shortly after 7 October 2023)

Silence

Silence makes its presence felt
In the stillness of the forest
Where the movement of a beetle
Scrabbling through autumn leaves
Sounds like a crack of thunder.

Silence makes its presence felt
When an audience is chattering loudly
But the speaker simply stands and waits,
No words needed to quieten the hubbub:
Their own silence as infectious as a cold.

Silence makes its presence felt
In the opaque darkness of a field
Where one stands longing for the moon
To light one's way, where one is isolated
In the nothingness of the night.

Silence makes its presence felt
In trauma and in tragedy
Where hands spin automatically to mouths
Stifling a gasp or scream of horror
A crowd brought together without words.

I lie in my bath

I lie in my bath, and I think of her,
many worlds away in Kiev,
where the air raid sirens blare
and drones endlessly circle overhead.

I lie in my bath, and I think of her,
as warm water laps round my knees,
and she lies cold in her bed,
no water, no heat, power, nor Wi-Fi.

I lie in my bath, and I think of her,
encircled by fear and farewells,
missiles and burnt-out buildings,
in her far-away country of the brave.

I lie in my bath, and I think of her,
filling mugs, bowls, pans and buckets
with water, when she's able,
watched by her son and Victory, the cat.

I lie in my bath and I think of her.
Her name does not trip off my tongue,
nor have we ever spoken,
but we are women, and know what love is.

I lie in my bath, and I think of her,
in the chill of snow and winter,
writing in the coffee shop,
where the generator gives her some warmth.

I lie in my bath, and I think of her,
in the city of grit and zeal,
and hope that she will be safe,
that her bath never fills with blood nor tears.

(Dedicated to Yaroslava Antipina, @strategywoman #warcoffee,
Resident of Kyiv, Ukraine. Published in Orbis)

Summer evening in Kew

It's 8 o'clock in the evening
The birds still sing
In the silhouette of the trees
A bat flies past
As if he knows where he's going
The trains whisk people home on the train
The planes overhead emit fatigue
As they hurry people back to their lives
After business trips or holidays
Frayed tempers, tired children.

Beethoven's Kreutzer Sonata
Plays all the while
Shedding its notes
Into the hydrangeas in my garden
The rosebuds and lilies
The scented rosemary and verbena
And as I sneeze
The birds sing a chorus of bless you
And goodnight
As dusk finally falls.

There's a lot of love about if you look for it

There's a lot of love about if you look in the right places
The quiet gaps of long-ago friendships that return
Around the corner from new friends
Who are just getting to know you.

In the rose that winks at you as it grows up your trellis
The random voice approaching from across the world on Twitter
The young girl who stands up for you on the train
The young child who smiles at you on the tube

The neighbour who offers to help when you're ill
The discussion that connects with your heart on the radio
And there's the cat as he purrs and massages his ears on your legs
It's all a love of sorts.

The desk in the corner of the room that reminds you of your
    mother's love
A painting of the South of France creating memories of happy times
The translucence of the dragonflies who show us that everything
    has a purpose
And us, we humans, play hide and seek with what we are here for.

The Dos and Don'ts of Poetry For a Teenager, from Vernon Scannell, 1966

Do write from direct experience.
Don't be too literary in your language.
Do use metaphors that delight the reader with a shock of poetic
  image.
Don't be predictable.

Don't confuse the role of the poet with a career.
Do realize no-one can make a living from writing poetry.
Don't worry if you never publish a line.
Do let your pen take to paper nonetheless.

Do practise your craft in all forms – write, write and write.
Don't forget also to read, read and read poetry.
Do realize there are ten charlatans for every genuine artist.
Don't be discouraged.

Do recognise that the profession of letters is exacting and
  disappointing.
Don't expect too much too quickly.
Do be patient and resilient to the apparent injustices.
Don't think true poetry is about spontaneous sincerity. This is
  nonsense.

Do sweat until your poems seem to have spontaneity.
Don't cease until they have the freshness of a thrush's song.
Do consider Yeats' saying that there is a "fascination of what is
  difficult".
Don't, in Coleridge's words, mistake a desire for reputation for the
  actual power of poetry.

Do avoid the huge abstractions, write simply using noun and verb.
Don't write loosely – "all those adjectives".
Do consider whether tranquillity can be anything but calm?
Don't lose the depth of feeling but, whatever you do, avoid the
word 'soul'.

(published as Advice to a Teenager in Orbis 177, 2016)

Frame-Change

She walked ghost galleries
of tortured faces;
Breughel and Bosch had nothing on this.
Her portrait hung with the caption
"Stupid".

Arrowed words sliced scars
of history and perception.
Stone cold burdens of her past
framed wet streets in shadow grey,
sneering fingers figured in unlit doorways;
a father's perspective tinting every lens.

Just one person's comment
at a moment in time:
his pinprick game to diminish her:
not the all-absorbing truth.
She hadn't thought of that.

Refocusing the frame,
she left her pigmy self
in rooms of childhood.
"I'll re-caption my portrait",
she whispered to the galleries of survivors,
"and rename my frame
Superwoman".

Fantasy Life

You were 26 years old,
witty, handsome.
You worked for a fashion brand
behind the Royal Academy,
relished a young man's London life.

After I heard the news I would lie in bed,
imagine not being able to feel my toes,
or move my legs,
pretend my arms were limp.
Wonder how that felt.

I would think of you every day for months
Wake and imagine being in a body
that didn't move below the neck.
Think of your parents
thinking of their son.

You would never walk again so they said,
a wheelchair for life,
carers 24/7,
a father embarrassed to be
the centre of such pity.

I lived your life but only in my mind.
A fantasy,
imagining myself in another's story,
as I do from time to time:
a bereaved parent, an orphaned child.

I was jolted back to myself the day you died.
I hadn't been the one
falling through that void of despair.
I'd only played with lost senses.
You'd lived the minutiae of hours within that leaden body.

The World has Changed, 2022

In a city square in Ukraine
prams are lined up
as if outside a children's party
or kindergarten, where mothers would wait.

But these mothers no longer wait
their lives are changed far beyond the screenshot.

There's no normality in this square.
Each pram and buggy is a symbol
of an innocent soul departed at the hands of the God of War,
Vladimir Putin.

On one pink buggy a pink teddy bear lies
propped up where a child should be.

A six-year old boy lies entubed in a hospital bed,
his face shattered by shrapnel.
The girl beside him has only one leg
the other blown away by a Russian bomb.

Her mother was cremated in front of her eyes
rendering her speechless for days.

In Poland tiny bundles of babies
saved from an orphanage,
lie on mattresses.

The world has changed.

Anthology

Who's that knocking?
The poets. And I, the listener,
open the door of my memory
to the sense of a book in my small hand,
the delight of being ill, off school,
a mild ailment, tucking myself in, under the cover.
I recollect the yellowing paper, a dry touch to my finger,
the smell of the pages sucking me in,
allowing me to lose myself,
spin scenes from the words.
Who's that knocking?
It started with Walter de la Mare.

What's that buzzing in my ears?
Jack Clemo's Christ in the Clay-Pit
that opened my eyes to the sacred.
The fading inscription from my parents
in *The Golden Treasury* that sits on my shelf,
a gift on my confirmation, aged fourteen.
The thumbed pages that flap open
to Byron, Lawrence, Wordsworth, Yeats.
Happy those early days when I read
but had not experienced the touch of a lover,
the pain of a parting with silence and tears.
I scour the pages now and ask, where was Blake?

Who's that knocking on the window,
pushing it open to consider the night,
to look at the stars, look at the skies?
Pascal, whose Pensees let in the light
to previously shuttered views of perception.
My father's gift, three shillings and sixpence.
Pascal's universe "an infinite sphere,
the centre of which is everywhere,

the circumference nowhere"
blowing my mind,
forcing me to reflect on infinity, on man with or without God.
About suffering he was not wrong.

Who's that pricking at my conscience?
The dusty blue book some fifty years old
still read, Pasternak, hammering always
the need for the heart of the matter,
the quest for a way, fame not a pretty sight,
success not your aim.
He the one who set my pen rolling
to emulate his words, his life
with my teenage poetry,
still shapes my words and views
whispers in my ear not to be an empty name
to defend my position, to be alive, myself.

Who's that crying?
I saw my infant son die a few weeks after he was born,
Charles Lamb's cradle-coffin verse of doom perverse beside me.
I shattered the cosiness of family life with divorce
yet the stars have not dealt me the worst they could do.
I have travelled among unknown men,
visited fifty countries or more, through heat and dust,
through ice and Arctic Circle; Yevtushenko's Russia,
Leopardi's Italy, Goethe's Germany,
and walked with Gibran in the Lebanon,
sat with Mary Oliver enjoying the sharpness of the morning
in New England. Seen that poets must loiter in green lanes.

Who's that knocking on the door?
The chattering of the beat poets
howling their way through the entrance in the garden wall,
while I hide beside the hollyhocks
with the Romantics at my side.
I re-read my early poems in their schoolgirl script,
interspersed with Vernon Scannell's notes in the margin,
laugh and cry with Copus and Cope,
leave Motion untouched in the bookcase,
switch off McGough on a Sunday afternoon,
and wonder, which poet will next direct my hand?

About the Author

Helen Whitten is a writer and prize-winning poet. She won Winchester Writers' Festival 2013 Poetry Prize and has won prizes in the Elmbridge Literary Festival Adult Poetry Prize 2014 and 2021. Her poems have been Highly Commended in the Elmbridge Literary Festival 2016 and the Winchester Writers' Festival 2014. Her first collection of poetry, *The Alchemist's Box* was published by Morgan's Eye Press in 2015, and on kindle by orrydian in 2024. Her poems have been published in journals and anthologies, including Orbis, Acumen, Loose Muse, South Bank Poetry, and the Winchester Writers' Festival Almanac.

Printed in Great Britain
by Amazon

53675212R00046